Table of Contents

Introduction

Reading comprehension is vital for success in school and for success in many other areas of life. To become confident, independent readers, children need to read with understanding and make sense of new words. Young readers need practice to strengthen their reading comprehension abilities.

The **Head for Home Reading** series provides additional practice with reading comprehension skills for readers at all ability levels. The selections in each workbook cover a wide range of high-interest topics and include both fiction and nonfiction texts.

Head for Home Reading: Grade 3 Intermediate is designed to reinforce reading comprehension skills by providing extra reading practice. The Intermediate level for grade 3 includes twelve lessons that target key reading skills. Each Intermediate lesson includes the following:

- An introduction defines the skill, explains why it is important, and provides step-by-step instructions for applying the skill

- A reading selection is followed by comprehension questions to check understanding and a graphic organizer to reinforce the skill.

By choosing this workbook, you are helping your child reinforce reading comprehension skills and achieve continued success in reading. A strong reading foundation will lead to a lifetime of reading enjoyment. Thank you for being involved in your child's learning. Here are a few suggestions for helping your child with reading comprehension.

- Read the instructions for each skill with your child. Preview the selection by looking at the title, images, and graphic organizer that follow.

- Help your child figure out the meaning of unfamiliar words through the context of the selection. Practice the new words with your child.

- Check the lesson when it is complete. Note areas of improvement and praise your child for success. Also note areas of concern and provide additional support as necessary.

Skill Focus: Characters

What are characters?

A **character** is a person or animal in a work of fiction. There is often more than one character in a story. We can use what a character says or the way a character looks and behaves to describe a character.

Why are characters important?

Identifying the characters in a story and understanding their actions and motives help us understand why the events in a story happen.

How to Understand Characters:

▸ Read the story.

▸ Identify the characters by underlining each character's name.

▸ Highlight the actions and events, or what the characters do in the story.

▸ Take notes about the motives, or reasons why a character does something in the story.

▸ Determine the cause of each action. Then determine the result of each action, or what happens.

▸ Write the key details about the character in a graphic organizer.

▸ Check your graphic organizer to make sure it tells about a character's actions and motivations, as well as the cause and result of each action.

Directions: Read the story once and answer the questions. Then, reread the story. Circle the name of one of the main characters. Underline that character's actions throughout the story.

The Magic Hat

¹Troy wanted to be a magician just like his father used to be. Now was a perfect time for Troy to be like his father. It was time for the school's talent show, and many students would try out, but only twenty-five would make it into the show. Troy decided that he wanted to do a magic show for the talent show tryouts. He knew he would need help, and he knew he would have to practice long and hard.

²"Dad, will you help me learn some new tricks for my magic show?" asked Troy.

³"Of course!" answered Dad. "But we need to get my old black magic hat from the closet to make you a real magician."

⁴"Can I wear it for tryouts?" asked Troy.

⁵"I think you will need to if you expect to pull a rabbit out of your hat," said Dad, laughing. He pulled down the dusty magic hat from the closet.

⁶"Do you think it will still work?" Troy asked.

⁷"Yes, it was the best magic hat I ever owned!" replied Dad.

⁸Dad and Troy began to practice tricks to do for the magic show. Dad taught Troy how to make objects disappear and then reappear. Troy was starting to feel ready for the talent show tryouts.

⁹"What if I don't make it into the talent show?" asked Troy.

¹⁰"Did you have fun learning how to do magic tricks?"

11 "Yes, I had the best time watching you and learning how to do some tricks myself," Troy answered.

12 "If you don't make it into the talent show, you did have fun trying," Dad explained.

13 "Yes, I guess you're right," said Troy. Troy gave his father a hug and smiled. His father always knew what to say to make him feel better.

14 A few days later, Troy ran up the front steps to the house, calling his father. "I made it, Dad, I made it! I'm in the talent show!" yelled Troy.

15 "I knew you could do it!" exclaimed Dad. "I can't wait to see you perform!"

16 "I couldn't have done it without you or your magic hat. Thank you so much, Dad," said Troy.

17 "You're welcome," replied Dad, and he held up a brand-new magic cape for Troy to put on.

Directions: Answer the questions.

1. Who are the main characters of the story?

_____

_____

_____

2. What are the characters doing in the story?

_____

_____

_____

_____

3. Why does Troy want to try out for the school's magic show?

_____

_____

_____

4. Why do you think Troy's father helps him?

_____

_____

_____

Directions: Use the graphic organizer to record information about one of the characters.

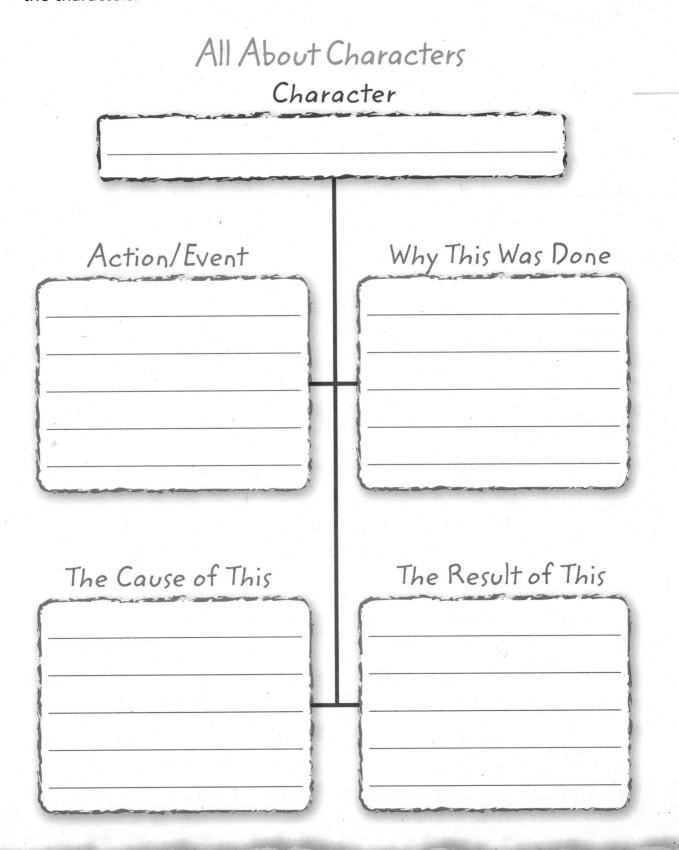

All About Characters

Character

Action/Event

Why This Was Done

The Cause of This

The Result of This

Skill Focus: Cause and Effect

What is cause and effect?

A **cause** is why something happens. An **effect** is the result of something that happens. For example, in a fictional story, a boy can fly *(effect)* because he is from another planet where everyone can fly *(cause)*.

Why is cause and effect important?

Being able to identify why something happens and its result helps us better understand what happens in a selection.

How to Identify Cause and Effect:

▸ Read the story.

▸ Think about the cause, or why something happens.

▸ Underline each cause in the story.

▸ Think about the effect, or result of something that happens.

▸ Circle each effect in the story.

▸ Write the causes and effects in a graphic organizer.

▸ Check your graphic organizer to make sure that the cause-and-effect relationship makes sense.

Directions: Read the story once and answer the questions. Then, reread the story. Underline each cause. Circle each effect.

Picking Up Trash

[1]It was a very windy day. Clothes hanging on lines danced in the wind, and leaves blew over the grass. Many other things, such as paper, cans, newspapers, and plastic bottles were blowing around in the neighborhood. Julio's mom gave him a bag and asked him to pick up the trash in the yard and then put it in a bin.

[2]In the front yard, the flagpole made a ringing sound as the rope slapped against it. Julio watched two birds on an overhead wire. They hung on tightly as the wind ruffled their feathers and rocked them on the wire.

[3]As fast as Julio picked up the trash, more blew into the yard. A green disc went rolling by. It had "B. J." written on it. *Brian Jackson,* Julio thought. He took the green disc over to Brian's house.

[4]Julio asked Brian if he wanted to help pick up the trash that was blowing around his yard. Brian wasn't sure at first, but Julio told him that it was fun. So he went with Julio.

[5]When they got to Julio's house, the two birds had just left the overhead wire. They flew down under a tree and up again. They did this again and again while chirping loudly. The boys looked under the tree and found a baby bird. "Maybe it fell out of the nest," said Brian.

⁶They could see the nest way above their heads. Brian didn't think the baby bird would be able to get back up there by itself in the strong wind.

⁷"I can reach the nest," said Julio. A tissue blew by, and he caught it. He took a paper cup from the trash bag. Using the tissue, Julio carefully picked up the baby bird and put it into the cup. "The bird's parents might not like me touching it with my hand," he said as he safely tucked the cup inside his shirt.

⁸As Julio climbed the tree, the birds flew around and around him. They seemed to be very nervous about where their baby was.

⁹It wasn't long before the two birds found their baby was safe in the nest. Then the two boys sat on the front step with the full trash bag. Brian told Julio that picking up trash was actually a lot of fun after all.

Directions: Answer the questions.

1. What effect does the wind have on Julio's yard?

_____

_____

_____

2. What caused the baby bird to end up under a tree?

_____

_____

_____

3. What caused Julio to go to Brian's house?

_____

_____

_____

4. What caused the two birds to be nervous?

_____

_____

_____

Cause and Effect
Head for Home Reading, Grade 3

Directions: Read the cause identified below. Use the graphic organizer to record three effects of that cause.

What Caused It? What Happens?

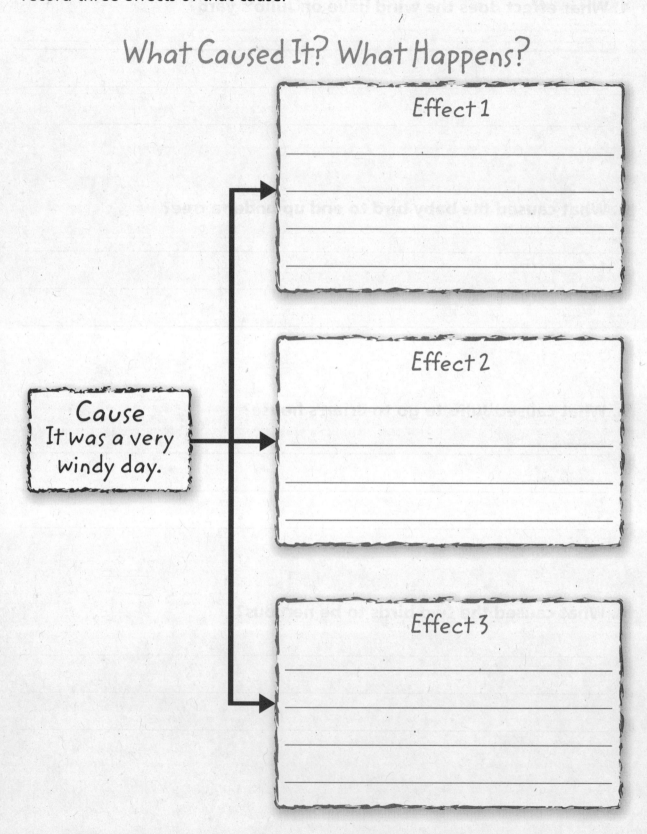

Effect 1

Effect 2

Cause
It was a very windy day.

Effect 3

Skill Focus: Main Idea and Details

What is a main idea? What is a detail?

A **main idea** is the most important idea in a selection. It tells what the selection is mostly about. The main idea is usually the first sentence in a selection. A **detail** supports or describes the selection's main idea.

Why are main ideas and details important?

Identifying and understanding the main idea and details helps us better comprehend the information in a selection.

How to Identify a Main Idea:

▸ Read the selection.

▸ Think about the most important idea as you read.

▸ Underline the main idea.

▸ Circle details that support the main idea.

▸ Write the main idea and details in a graphic organizer.

▸ Check your graphic organizer to make sure you state the main idea and details clearly.

Directions: Read the selection once and answer the questions. Then, reread the selection. Underline the selection's main idea. Circle each supporting detail.

Insect-eating Plant

¹The Venus's flytrap is one kind of insect-eating plant. It is found in bogs, or wet, spongy land in North and South Carolina.

²The leaves form a hinged trap. When a fly lands on it, the leaf snaps shut, trapping the fly inside. The trap will shut in less than a second! The trap stays closed for five to ten days while the plant eats the insect. Then the leaf opens and it is ready for more insects.

³People are excited about having this plant. Now many greenhouses in the United States grow them for people to buy. If you'd like to own a Venus's flytrap, check with your local nursery or search for sellers online.

Directions: Answer the questions.

1. What is the main idea of the selection?

A. The Venus's-flytrap has leaves that form a hinged trap.

B. The Venus's-flytrap is one kind of insect-eating plant.

C. The Venus's-flytrap is found in North and South Carolina.

2. What is a detail that supports the main idea of the selection?

A. The trap stays closed for five to ten days while the plant eats the insect.

B. People are excited about having this kind of plant.

C. Now many greenhouses in the United States grow them for people to buy.

3. What sentence is NOT a detail that supports the main idea?

A. When a fly lands on it, the leaf snaps shut, trapping the fly inside.

B. It is found in bogs, or wet, spongy land.

C. If you'd like to own a Venus's flytrap, check with your local nursery or search for sellers online.

Directions: Write the selection's main idea and supporting details in this graphic organizer.

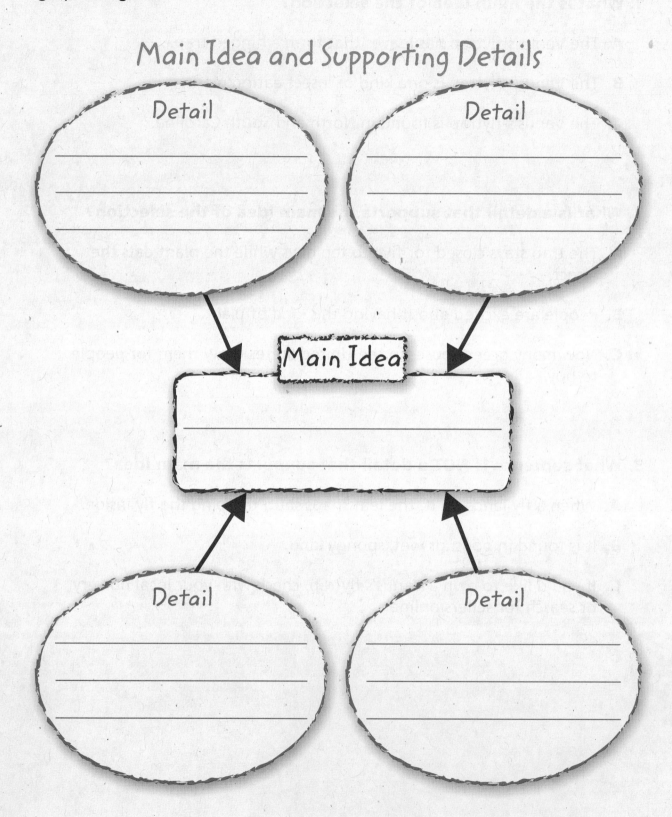

Main Idea and Supporting Details

Detail

Detail

Main Idea

Detail

Detail

Directions: Write a paragraph about your favorite plant and what you like about it. Be sure your paragraph includes a main idea and three details that support it. Begin your paragraph with the main idea.

My Favorite Plant

_____

_____

_____

_____

_____

_____

_____

_____

_____

_____

_____

_____

_____

_____

_____

_____

_____

Skill Focus: Plot

What is plot?

A **plot** is the storyline, or main story of a literary work, such as a short story, play, or novel. The plot includes a series, or sequence, of events that take place and tell what happens in the story.

Why is plot important?

The plot helps us understand the characters' motives and actions. Understanding the plot helps us understand the characters and the choices they make. It also helps us understand the events that happen before and after other events in the story.

How to Understand Plot:

▸ Read the story.

▸ Identify the main character by circling the character's name.

▸ Ask yourself questions about the sequence of events that happen in the story, such as: *What happens first in the story? What happens next? Then what happens? What happens last in the story?*

▸ Highlight or underline the main events.

▸ Write each event in the correct sequence in a graphic organizer.

▸ Check your graphic organizer to make sure that you have written the series of events in the proper sequence, or order, in which each event happens.

Directions: Read the story once and answer the questions. Then, reread the story. Underline the main plot events.

Watusi Wins the Race

[1]Watusi was the smallest person in the entire third grade. He was embarrassed because he was so small, and he had to stand on a step stool to sharpen his pencil in class.

[2]Watusi liked school, except for outside recess. He tried to play basketball, but he was too small to guard anybody. He then tried to play football, but his hands were too small to catch the ball. After that, he tried to play baseball, but the baseball glove fell off his hand. Finally, his classmates tried to get him to jump rope, but they got tired of having to bend down low so that Watusi could jump.

[3]One day, Watusi's teacher told the class that they would be participating in a race. The fastest student would get to represent the school in a big race against students from other schools. That day at recess all the students raced each other to see who was the fastest. Watusi just sat down on a bench and watched.

[4]"Why aren't you racing?" asked Watusi's teacher.

[5]"I'm too small," said Watusi.

[6]"Try it." Watusi's teacher smiled. "You might be surprised."

[7]Watusi decided to run in the next race. When Watusi's teacher said, "Go!" Watusi ran as fast as he could. He did not think about being too small. All he thought about was how good the wind felt against his face. He did not even think about his opponents. He just ran.

[8]Watusi heard his classmates cheering. He saw that he was at the finish line. He won! This happened each time Watusi raced. At the end of the week, his teacher told the class that Watusi would represent their school in the district races.

[9]The end of the week came, and it was time for Watusi's race. He was nervous as he stood at the starting line. There were a lot of people in the crowd. All the third-grade students in his class were cheering for him.

[10]Watusi looked at the other students running in his race. Once again, he was the smallest in the group.

[11]When the signal was given, Watusi ran as fast as he could. He did not think about being too small. He thought about how good the wind felt in his face. Watusi reached the finish line. Watusi won the race. He felt proud as the district superintendent gave him a medal. Never again would he feel that he was too small to do anything.

Directions: Answer the questions.

1. Which of the following events happened first?

    A. Watusi ran in a big race at school.

    B. Watusi sat down on a bench and watched the other kids race.

    C. The teacher told the class that they would be participating in a race.

2. Which of the following events happened right after the big race began?

    A. Watusi was first at the finish line.

    B. Watusi heard his classmates cheering.

    C. Watusi ran as fast as he could.

3. Which of the following events happened last?

    A. The superintendent gave Watusi a medal.

    B. Watusi won the district race.

    C. Watusi ran as fast as he could when the signal was given.

Directions: Use the graphic organizer to record the plot's main events.

Putting Plot Events in Order

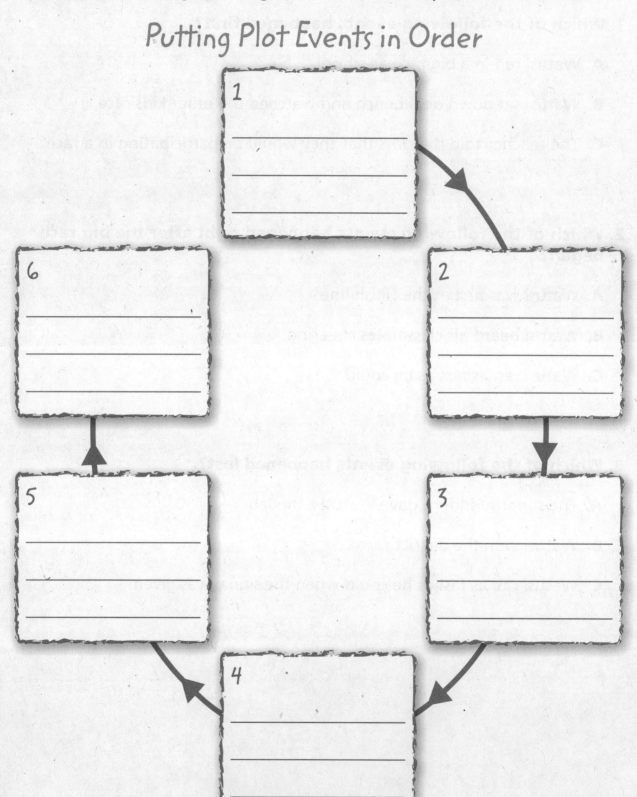

Skill Focus: Problem and Resolution

What is a problem? What is a resolution?

A **problem** is an issue that a character or characters must deal with and solve in a story. A **resolution** is how a character's problem is solved, or worked out, in a story.

Why is resolving a problem important?

Identifying a problem and how it is resolved helps us understand the important elements of a story.

How to Understand Problem and Resolution:

▸ Read the story.

▸ Identify the main characters by highlighting each character's name.

▸ Circle the problem that the main characters have.

▸ Underline how the main characters resolve the problem.

▸ Think about and highlight what happens when the problem is solved.

▸ Write the information in a graphic organizer.

▸ Check your graphic organizer to make sure it tells about a problem, the resolution to the problem, and what happens when the problem is solved.

Directions: Read the story once and answer the questions. Then, reread the story. Circle a problem the main characters have. Underline the resolution.

Summer Camp Treasure

[1]Harry and Harriet were twins, and they loved going to summer camp in the mountains. While they enjoyed horseback riding, swimming, and playing ball, their favorite part about summer camp was trying to find buried treasure using a map. Pairs of children always teamed up on the last day of camp to try to find the hidden treasure. This year, Harry and Harriet wanted to be the first ones to find it.

[2]"Remember, teams, work together and good luck!" said Mr. Garcia, the camp counselor.

[3]The children scattered in all directions. The twins quickly looked at their map.

[4]"I think we need to head east," said Harry.

[5]"Let's go," said Harriet. They started walking east.

[6]"It should be right here under this tree," said Harry, pointing at a large pine.

[7]They began to dig and dig.

[8]"That's odd. No treasure," said Harry.

[9]"It *has* to be here," said Harriet. She looked at the map again. Just then, Harry realized that the map was turned the wrong way.

[10]"Wait!" he exclaimed. "The treasure is hidden under the *west* tree."

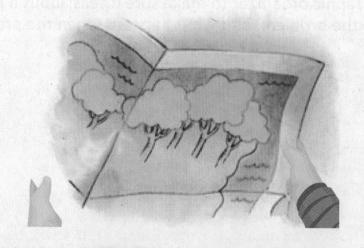

¹¹They ran to the west end of the camp and found the tree on the map. They dug as fast as they could. After a few minutes, Harry struck something hard.

¹²"We found it!" he shouted.

¹³They pulled a wooden treasure chest from the dirt and raced back to their camp counselor.

¹⁴"Congratulations! You found it first," said Mr. Garcia. "Here's the key to open your treasure."

¹⁵The other children looked on, and Harriet took the key. She opened the treasure chest. Inside were two action figures wrapped in shiny paper.

¹⁶"Wow! This is great!" said Harry.

¹⁷Later that day, the twins went home on the bus feeling very happy about their time at camp. They could not wait to tell their parents that they had found the buried treasure this year.

Directions: Answer the questions.

1. Who are the main characters of the story?

_____

_____

_____

2. What are they doing in the woods?

_____

_____

_____

3. Why couldn't the main characters find the treasure at first?

_____

_____

_____

_____

4. How do the main characters feel at the end of the story? Why?

_____

_____

_____

_____

Directions: Use the graphic organizer to record information about the problem and resolution in the story.

What's the Problem?
What is the main problem in the story?

_____
_____
_____
_____

How is the problem solved?

_____
_____
_____
_____

What happens when the problem is solved?

_____
_____
_____
_____

Skill Focus: Prefixes and Suffixes

What is a prefix? What is a suffix?

A **prefix** is a word part added to the beginning of a word to form a new word with a new meaning. The prefix *un-* means "not" or "the opposite of." The word *unable* means "not able."

A **suffix** is a word part added to the end of a word to form a new word with a new meaning. The suffix *-ed* can be added to a word to show an action has already happened, or it can mean "having the characteristic of." The word *looked* means "to have seen."

Why are knowing the meanings of prefixes and suffixes important?

Understanding the meanings of prefixes and suffixes helps us understand the meaning of unfamiliar words. It also helps us understand what we are reading.

How to Identify Prefixes and Suffixes:

▸ Read the selection.

▸ Circle each word with a prefix. First, identify the meaning of the prefix. Then, identify the meaning of the entire word.

▸ Underline each word with a suffix. First, identify the meaning of the suffix. Then, identify the meaning of the entire word.

▸ Write each word in a graphic organizer.

▸ Check your graphic organizer to make sure that you have correctly identified the prefixes and suffixes as well as each word's meaning.

Directions: Read the story once and answer the questions. Then, reread the story. Circle words with prefixes. Underline words with suffixes.

Uneasy Feelings

¹Hakeem sometimes had problems falling asleep. Tonight was one of those times. The next day was the monthly math test, and that made him very nervous. He was worried that he might make a mistake. Last month he miscopied a few problems and redrew the wrong triangle.

²Usually Hakeem fell asleep quickly. But when he was nervous, he felt afraid of the darkness. He would stay awake and see shadows on his walls. The shadows looked like scary people from a bad dream. Hakeem knew they were just the shadows from the trees in the backyard. But he couldn't avoid worrying about the possibilities.

³All of a sudden, Hakeem heard an unusual noise beating against his windows. He didn't want to call his mom. So he just pulled the covers over his head. Then Hakeem heard the noise again. Sleeping upstairs could be so scary! He listened more carefully. He would need a bloodhound to figure out this mystery! *I have to get some sleep*, thought Hakeem. *If I don't do well on the test, I'll have to retake it.*

⁴Hakeem tried to sleep, but it seemed that the noise grew louder. He buried his face in his pillowcase. Was something trying to get in through his window? A loud knock on Hakeem's door made him leap out of bed. It was only his mom. She said, "I'm sorry about all that noise. I think that we're going to get a bad storm." She told Hakeem not to worry about the test because he studied hard. She left the hallway light on until Hakeem finally fell asleep.

Prefixes and Suffixes
Head for Home Reading, Grade 3

Directions: Answer the questions.

1. What word has a prefix?

   A. untie

   B. pulled

   C. sleeping

2. What word has a suffix?

   A. preplan

   B. proactive

   C. tearful

3. What does the word *redo* mean?

   A. "to do"

   B. "to do again"

   C. "to not do again"

4. Which of the following words means "not friendly"?

   A. friendless

   B. unfriendly

   C. refriendly

Directions: Use the graphic organizer to record information about word parts. Use a dictionary if you need to check the meaning of a word.

Add a Word Part & Change the Meaning!

Prefix/Suffix	Word	Meaning

Prefixes and Suffixes
Head for Home Reading, Grade 3

Directions: Read the words and write them in the correct column. Then, use each word in a sentence.

| misfire | jumped | higher | precook | biggest |
| redress | unfriendly | running | quickly | proactive |

Sort and Write

Words with a Prefix	Words with a Suffix
_____	_____
_____	_____
_____	_____
_____	_____
_____	_____
_____	_____
_____	_____
_____	_____
_____	_____
_____	_____
_____	_____
_____	_____
_____	_____

Skill Focus: Author's Purpose

What is an author's purpose?

An author writes a selection to persuade, to inform, or to entertain. These reasons are called the **author's purpose**.

For example, an author might write to persuade, or convince readers of something. When the author wants to inform readers, he or she has information to tell. Sometimes an author wants readers to enjoy the writing. In this case, the author writes to entertain his or her audience.

Why is knowing an author's purpose important?

Identifying the author's purpose helps us understand the main idea and important details of a selection.

How to Identify an Author's Purpose:

▸ Read the selection.

▸ Ask yourself whether the author is writing to persuade, to inform, or to entertain readers.

▸ Highlight details that support the author's purpose.

▸ Write the author's purpose and details that support it in a graphic organizer.

Directions: Read each selection once. Below each, write whether the author's purpose is to persuade, inform, or entertain. Then reread the selections and answer the questions.

The Three R's

¹We can help manage how much waste or trash we make by following the three R's—*reduce, reuse,* and *recycle.* Following these rules will help us to make less trash.

²*Reduce* means to use less. We need to use fewer things that make trash.

³*Reuse* means to take things you would usually throw away and find ways to use them again. Many people reuse cardboard boxes, plastic bags, grocery bags, newspapers, and glass jars.

⁴*Recycle* means to treat the trash so that we can use it again. Some of the things people recycle are aluminum, glass, paper, and plastic. These things can be used again to make a different product.

The author's purpose is to

_____

_____

Tops Toothpaste

[1]Do you want whiter teeth? Do you want cleaner teeth? Do you want fresher breath?

[2]Then you need to buy a tube of Tops Toothpaste. Tops Toothpaste will make your teeth whiter. Tops Toothpaste will make your teeth feel cleaner. Tops Toothpaste will make your breath smell fresher.

The author's purpose is to

_____

_____

_____

_____

Paul Bunyan

[1]Paul Bunyan was so big that he could not fit inside most people's houses. He would have to talk with people outside. One day he went to visit some friends outside their house. Then it began to rain. Paul Bunyan pulled the roof off their house. He held the roof over everyone like a huge umbrella.

The author's purpose is to

_____

_____

_____

_____

Author's Purpose
Head for Home Reading, Grade 3

Directions: Answer the questions.

1. Write one fact from "The Three R's."

_____

_____

_____

_____

2. How does the author of "Tops Toothpaste" try to convince the reader to buy this kind of toothpaste?

_____

_____

_____

_____

3. What is entertaining about reading "Paul Bunyan"?

_____

_____

_____

_____

Directions: Choose one of the selections. Use the graphic organizer to record details about it.

Title of Selection: _____

Detail 1:
_____
_____
_____

Detail 2:
_____
_____
_____

Author's Purpose:
_____
_____

Detail 3:
_____
_____
_____

Skill Focus: Setting

What is setting?

A **setting** is where and when a story takes place. A setting sets up the actions and events in a story. The setting can affect what the characters do in the story. A story can have more than one setting.

Why is setting important?

A setting is important to a story's meaning because it tells where and when all of the events in a story take place. Setting can also explain the reasons for a character's actions. For readers, it can help us to more fully understand what is happening in the story.

How to Understand Setting:

▸ Read the story.

▸ Identify where the story takes place by underlining this information.

▸ Identify when the story takes place by circling this information.

▸ Think about and determine how the setting is important to the story.

▸ Write this information in a graphic organizer.

▸ Check your graphic organizer to make sure that you have identified where and when the story takes place, and why the setting is important.

Directions: Read the story once. Then, reread the story and highlight information that tells where and when the story takes place.

A Steel-Driving Man

[1] John Henry was a hard-working man. Although he had been a slave in the South, he was freed after the Civil War. He went to work as a steel-driver for the railroad. The other railroad workers called John the fastest and most powerful man they had ever seen working.

[2] Every day, John went to work hitting steel spikes into the rocks. Soon miles and miles of shiny new track were laid. Now there were tracks where only dirt had been before. The men said that John was so fast and powerful that he could do twice as much work as most men.

[3] Progress on laying the railroad track was coming along quite well. Finally, John and the construction crew reached Big Bend Mountain in West Virginia. The mountain was wide and thick. The railroad foremen knew that the mountain was too large to go around. So they called the crew together. The crew was told that they would have to dig straight through the huge mountain.

[4] John Henry just smiled. He told the bosses that getting through that big ole mountain would be as easy as cutting through butter. John went to work hammering away, digging right through the mountain.

[5] The next day, a salesman came into camp with a new powerful drill. He said his drill would be able to move through that big ole mountain ten times faster than any man. He told the bosses that, with his drills, they would have themselves a tunnel through the mountain in no time at all. The other railroad workers all laughed. They said that no drill could ever beat the fast and mighty swings of John Henry.

[6]To prove the point, the men suggested having a contest between John and the fancy drill. John laughingly accepted. All the men stopped work to cheer their favorite hero on against the fancy power drill.

[7]One of the bosses agreed to run the drill, and the contest began. John's hammers flew like lightning. Bang! Clang! The power drill whirled and sputtered along. It was biting away at the mountain like a hungry animal. The men cheered and yelled while the dust whirled and swirled. At the end of the time, John had worked his way fourteen feet into the huge mountain! The drill had only gone nine feet! The men stomped their feet and whooped! John had beaten the fancy drill, hands down!

[8]Everyone was so busy celebrating that they didn't notice John fall to the ground. All of a sudden someone yelled, "Get help!" But it was too late. The mighty man had beaten the power drill. But the effort had been too much for him. He died on the spot.

[9]Even without John, the men finally cut through Big Bend Mountain and laid the shiny railroad track. But it is said that on a quiet night, if you listen carefully, you can still hear John hammering away inside the tunnels of Big Bend Mountain.

Directions: Answer the questions.

1. Which of the following is NOT part of the setting?

    A. West Virginia

    B. Big Bend Mountain

    C. the South

2. When does the story take place?

    A. before the Civil War

    B. during the Civil War

    C. after the Civil War

3. Why is John Henry known as a "steel-driving man"?

    A. He was big and powerful.

    B. He could hit thick steel spikes into rocks.

    C. He said that getting through the mountain would be as easy as cutting through butter.

Directions: Use the graphic organizer to record information about the story's setting.

The Setting

Where Does the Story Take Place?

_____
_____
_____
_____
_____
_____

When Does the Story Take Place?

_____
_____
_____
_____
_____
_____

How Is the Setting Important to the Story's Meaning?

_____
_____
_____
_____
_____
_____
_____

Skill Focus: Fact and Opinion

What is a fact? What is an opinion?

A **fact** is information that can be proven to be true. An **opinion** is a thought or feeling about a topic. Phrases such as *I think, I believe, my favorite, the most,* and *the best* help you identify a statement of opinion.

Why is knowing the difference between facts and opinions important?

Authors often include both facts and opinions in their writing. Understanding the difference between facts and opinions helps us identify when a statement is true and when a statement is the author's feelings about the subject.

How to Distinguish Between Facts and Opinions:

▸ Read the selection.

▸ Think about whether a statement can be proven true. Ask yourself questions, such as: *Can this statement be proven to be true? Does this statement tell how the author feels about the subject? Does the statement begin with* I think, I believe, *or* My favorite?

▸ Underline each fact.

▸ Circle each opinion.

▸ Write the facts and opinions in a graphic organizer.

▸ Check your graphic organizer to make sure you have written the information under the correct category.

Directions: Read the passage once and answer the questions. Then, reread the passage. Underline each fact. Circle each opinion.

The Black Rhinoceros

[1]The black rhinoceros has thick, gray skin. It has two horns. The rhino's horns are made of the same material as its toenails. The front horn can grow to over one foot in length. I think a horn would be strange to have on one's face. An adult rhino weighs between 2,000 and 3,000 pounds. It grows 10 to 12 feet long. The black rhino has a good sense of smell and excellent hearing but very poor eyesight. Its average lifespan is 40 years. The black rhinoceros is now on the endangered animal list. Today there are fewer than 3,000 black rhinos. I believe we need to save the black rhino from disappearing.

Directions: Answer the questions.

1. Which of the following is a fact about the black rhinoceros?

    A. I think a horn would be strange to have on one's face.

    B. The front horn can grow to over one foot in length.

    C. I believe we need to save the black rhino from disappearing.

2. Which of the following is an opinion about the black rhinoceros?

    A. The rhino's horns are made of the same material as its toenails.

    B. The black rhinoceros is now on the endangered animal list.

    C. I think a horn would be strange to have on one's face.

3. Which of the following sentences is NOT a fact?

    A. The black rhino is an interesting animal.

    B. The black rhino has thick, gray skin.

    C. The black rhino has two horns.

Directions: Write a sentence in the top box describing the selection's topic. Then write facts and opinions in the correct columns.

Fact or Opinion?

Fact   Opinion

Directions: Read the following statements. On the lines, write whether each statement is a *fact* or an *opinion*.

You Decide!

1. Elephants can weigh up to 15,000 pounds.

_____

_____

_____

2. Elephants are the most amazing mammals.

_____

_____

_____

3. The best place to see an elephant is at the zoo.

_____

_____

_____

4. I believe all elephants should be left in their natural environments.

_____

_____

_____

5. Elephants do not live as long in zoos as they do in the wild.

_____

_____

_____

6. In the wild, elephants may walk as far as 50 miles in one day.

_____

_____

_____

Skill Focus: Point of View

What is point of view?

Point of view is the perspective from which a story is told. An author can tell a story in a first-person point of view. In this point of view, the person telling the story is a character in the story. The author uses words such as *I* and *me*. An author can also tell a story in a third-person point of view. In this point of view, the person telling the story is not a character in the story. The author uses words such as *he*, *she*, and *they*.

Why is knowing the point of view important?

Knowing who is telling the story, or the point of view, helps us understand what happens in the story.

How to Identify the Author's Point of View:

▸ Read the story.

▸ Ask yourself questions about the story's point of view, such as: *Is the main character telling the story? Does the narrator use the pronouns I or me? Does the narrator use the pronouns* he, she, *or* they?

▸ Circle words that give you clues about the story's point of view.

Directions: Read the passage once and answer the questions. Then, reread the story. Circle words that give you clues about the author's point of view.

Johnny Appleseed

[1]John Chapman was born in 1774 and grew up in Massachusetts. He became a farmer who grew different types of crops and trees. John mainly liked to grow and eat apples. Many people were moving west at that time. They were going toward Ohio. John knew that apples were a good food for people to have. Apple trees were strong and easy to grow. Apples could be eaten raw or cooked in many ways. In 1797, John headed west. He planted apple seeds as he went along. He also gave apple seeds to people who wanted to grow apple trees by their homes. The people nicknamed him Johnny Appleseed. Thanks to Johnny Appleseed, apple trees grow in the United States where they once never did.

Directions: Answer the questions.

1. Which word or words in the following sentence give you clues about the point of view: *He planted apple seeds as he went along.*

_____

_____

_____

_____

_____

2. Which word or words in the following sentence give you clues about the point of view: *John knew that apples were a good food for people to have.*

_____

_____

_____

_____

_____

3. What point of view does the author use?

_____

_____

_____

_____

_____

Directions: Read each sentence. Then, complete the chart.

Clues to Point of View

	Point of View	Clue Words
1. My name is John Chapman.		
2. He became a farmer who grew trees.		
3. I knew that apples were a good food for people to have.		
4. I headed west in 1797.		
5. In 1797, John headed west.		
6. People nicknamed me Johnny Appleseed.		
7. He gave apple seeds to people who wanted to grow apple trees.		
8. Thanks to him, apple trees grow in the United States where they once never did.		

Directions: Reread "Johnny Appleseed." Rewrite the story using a first-person point of view.

The Story of Me: Johnny Appleseed!

_____

_____

_____

_____

_____

_____

_____

_____

_____

_____

_____

_____

_____

Skill Focus: Retell

What is a retell?

When we **retell** a story, we are using our own words to tell the story again.

Why is retelling important?

Being able to retell a story is an important skill because it helps us to remember, talk about, and understand what we read.

How to Retell a Story:

▸ Read the selection.

▸ Identify the important parts of the selection by underlining them.

▸ Retell the events in order, in your own words, using words such as *first, next, then,* and *last.*

▸ Write the retelling on a graphic organizer.

▸ Draw pictures to help you remember each important part of the story.

▸ Check your graphic organizer to make sure you have put the events in the correct order.

Directions: Read the story once and answer the questions. Then, reread the story. Underline the important parts of the story.

A New Home

[1]The puppy sat in the enclosure at the animal shelter with all of the other dogs. She was smaller than the other dogs because she was just a puppy. She was too young to know what was really going on, so she sat in the corner quietly.

[2]The puppy could see many people walking by. Then she saw a man she thought would be a good friend. When the man looked in the enclosure she made a jump for the front. She landed on top of the other dogs. She began pushing them aside, even though they were all much bigger. She wagged her tail with excitement and licked the hand of the man who had reached down to pet her and the other dogs.

[3]The moment the man saw this puppy he knew this was the dog he was going to take home. The man named her Obie, which was short for obnoxious. The puppy seemed to know she was the perfect dog and would do anything to be seen!

Directions: Answer the questions.

1. What happened first in the story?

   A. A puppy saw a man she thought would be a good friend.

   B. The puppy jumped over other dogs to get closer to the man.

   C. The puppy sat quietly in the corner of an enclosure at the animal shelter.

2. Right after the puppy saw the man, she

   A. jumped over the other dogs.

   B. wagged her tail.

   C. licked the man's hand.

3. What happened last in the story?

   A. The puppy wagged her tail and licked the man's hand.

   B. The man named the dog Obie.

   C. The puppy landed on the other dogs.

Directions: Use words and pictures to record important events from the story. Use words such as *first, next, then,* and *last* to tell about what is happening in each picture. Then write a number in the corner of each picture to show the sequence.

Telling It My Way!

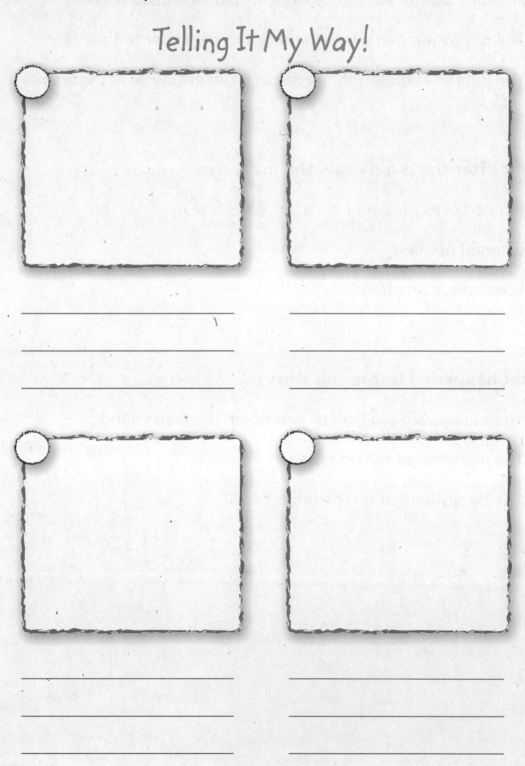

Skill Focus: Summarize

What is summarizing?

When we **summarize**, we tell the most important ideas and details of a selection, leaving out unnecessary information.

Why is summarizing important?

Summarizing is an important skill to learn because it helps us to remember what we read. When we summarize, we tell what we learned from a selection, including only the most important information.

How to Write a Good Summary:

▸ Read the selection.

▸ Identify the main idea and underline it.

▸ Circle details that support the main idea.

▸ Write a summary on a graphic organizer, using your own words. Include only the most important information.

▸ Check your summary to make sure it tells only the most important ideas in the selection.

Directions: Read the passage once and answer the questions. Then, reread the passage. Underline the important information in the story.

CALL 911

[1]The number 911 is a special phone number that has been set up for emergencies. If you need help right away, you can call 911. The operator will ask you for your name and address. The operator will ask you what the problem is. Then the operator will send the police, an ambulance, and, if necessary, the fire department to your address. If your town doesn't have a 911 system, you may dial "0." Many lives have been saved by people calling 911 quickly in an emergency.

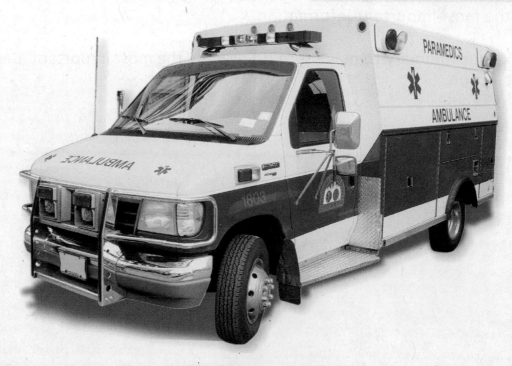

Directions: Answer the questions.

1. What is the main idea of the selection?

_____

_____

_____

_____

2. What is an important detail that supports the main idea?

_____

_____

_____

_____

3. What is one detail you would leave out of a summary of the selection?

_____

_____

_____

_____

Directions: Use the graphic organizer to record the main idea and supporting details from the selection. Then write a summary.

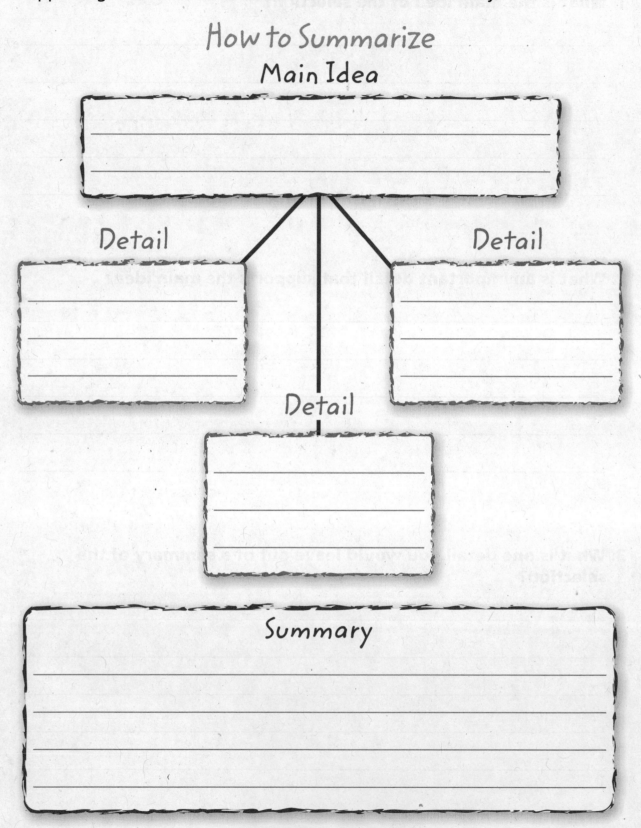

How to Summarize

Main Idea

_____

_____

Detail

_____

_____

Detail

_____

_____

Detail

_____

_____

Summary

_____

_____

_____

_____

Answer Key

Characters, pp. 3–7
Selection: The Magic Hat, p. 6

1. Troy and his father
2. Troy's father is teaching Troy magic tricks so Troy can try out for the talent show.
3. Troy wants to be a magician, just like his father used to be.
4. Possible answer: Troy's dad loves his son and wants him to be successful and happy.

Graphic Organizer: All About Characters, p. 7

Possible answer:
Character: Troy
Action/Event: Troy asks his father for help learning new magic tricks.
Why This Was Done: Troy wants to learn new tricks for his act in the talent show.
The Cause of This: He doesn't know a lot of magic tricks. He wants to be in the talent show.
The Result of This: Troy learns many magic tricks from his father and gets into the talent show.

Cause and Effect, pp. 8–12
Selection: Picking Up Trash, p. 11

1. The wind left Julio's yard messy with trash from around the neighborhood.
2. The baby bird probably fell to the ground when a gust of wind blew.
3. Julio thought the disc belonged to Brian, so Julio took it to Brian's house.
4. The two birds were nervous because the baby bird was not in the nest.

Graphic Organizer: What Caused It? What Happens? p. 12

Possible answers:
Effect 1: Trash blew around the neighborhood.
Effect 2: Julio's mom asked him to pick up trash in the yard.
Effect 3: A baby bird fell from its nest.

Main Idea and Details, pp. 13–17
Selection: Insect-eating Plant, p. 15

1. B
2. A
3. C

Graphic Organizer: Main Idea and Supporting Details, p. 16

Main Idea: The Venus's-flytrap is one kind of insect-eating plant.
Detail: It is found in bogs in North and South Carolina.
Detail: The leaves trap insects.
Detail: The plant takes five to ten days to eat an insect.
Detail: The leaves open after the insect is eaten.

Practice, p. 17
Possible answer:
My favorite plant is an oak tree. I like oak trees because they get big and make shade. I also like oak trees because they make acorns that animals eat. Oak trees also make good homes for animals like squirrels and birds.

Plot, pp. 18–22

1. C
2. C
3. A

Graphic Organizer: Putting Plot Events in Order, p. 22
1. Watusi doesn't like recess because he is too small to be good at sports.
2. Watusi's teacher announces a school race.
3. Watusi runs in the school race and wins.
4. Watusi represents his school in the district races.
5. Watusi wins his race.
6. Watusi receives a medal.

Problem and Resolution, pp. 23–27
Selection: Summer Camp Treasure, p. 26

1. Harry and Harriet
2. They are looking for a buried treasure.
3. They were holding the map the wrong way.
4. Harry and Harriet were happy because they found the buried treasure.

Graphic Organizer: What's the Problem? p. 27

What is the main problem in the story? Harry and Harriet want to be the first campers to find the buried treasure.

How is the problem solved? The twins turn the map and realize that the treasure is hidden under the west tree, not the east tree.

What happens when the problem is solved? The twins are happy because they will share their treasure with each other.

Prefixes and Suffixes, pp. 28–32
Selection: Uneasy Feelings, p. 30

1. A
2. C
3. B
4. B

Graphic Organizer: Add a Word Part & Change the Meaning! p. 31

Possible answers: mis-/miscopied/"to not copy correctly"; re-/redrew/"to draw again"; -ly/quickly/"in a quick way"; -ness/darkness/"being dark"; un-/unusual/"not usual"

Practice, p. 32

Prefix: misfire, precook, redress, unfriendly, proactive
Suffix: jumped, higher, biggest, unfriendly, running, quickly

Author's Purpose, pp. 33–37
Selections: The Three R's, Tops Toothpaste, Paul Bunyan, pp. 34–36

The Three R's: The author's purpose is to inform.
Tops Toothpaste: The author's purpose is to persuade.
Paul Bunyan: The author's purpose is to entertain.

1. Possible answer: We can help manage how much waste or trash we make by following the three R's: *reduce, reuse,* and *recycle.*
2. Possible answer: By saying it will do things such as make my breath smell fresher.
3. Possible answer: The story about Paul Bunyan is entertaining because it couldn't really happen. For example, Paul Bunyan is so big and strong that he can pull a roof off of a house and use it like an umbrella.

Graphic Organizer, p. 37

Possible answer:
Title: Tops Toothpaste
Author's Purpose: to persuade
Detail 1: It will make your teeth whiter.
Detail 2: It will make your teeth feel cleaner.
Detail 3: It will make your breath smell fresher.

Setting, pp. 38–42
Selection: A Steel-Driving Man, p. 41

1. C
2. C
3. B

Graphic Organizer: The Setting, p. 42

Where does the story take place? Big Bend Mountain; West Virginia

When does the story take place? after the Civil War

How is the setting important to the story? The difficulty of going through a mountainside setting shows how powerful and strong John Henry was.

Fact and Opinion, pp. 43–47
Selection: The Black Rhinoceros, p. 45

1. B
2. C
3. A

Graphic Organizer: Fact or Opinion? p. 46

Possible answers:

Facts:
The black rhinoceros has thick, gray skin; It has two horns; The rhino's horns are made of the same material as its toenails; The front horn can grow to over one foot in length.

Opinions:
I think a horn would be strange to have on one's face; I believe we need to save the black rhino from disappearing.

Practice, p. 47

1. fact
2. opinion
3. opinion
4. opinion
5. fact
6. fact

Point of View, pp. 48–52
Selection: Johnny Appleseed, p. 50

1. *he*
2. *John*
3. third person

Graphic Organizer: Clues to Point of View, p. 51

1. first; *my*
2. third; *he*
3. first; *I*
4. first; *I*

5. third; *John*
6. first; *me*
7. third; *he*
8. third; *him*

Practice, p. 52

Possible response:

My name is John Chapman. I was born in 1774 and grew up in Massachusetts. I became a farmer who grew different types of crops and trees. I mainly liked to grow and eat apples. Many people were moving west at that time. They were going toward Ohio. I knew that apples were a good food for people to have. Apple trees were strong and easy to grow. Apples could be eaten raw or cooked in many ways. In 1797, I headed west. I planted apple seeds as I went along. I also gave my apple seeds to people who wanted to grow apple trees by their homes. The people nicknamed me Johnny Appleseed. Thanks to me, apple trees started to grow in the United States where they once never did.

Retell, pp. 53–56
Selection: A New Home, p. 55

1. C
2. A
3. B

Graphic Organizer: Telling It My Way! p. 56

Possible answer:

1. First, the puppy sat quietly in a corner.
2. Next, the puppy saw a man she liked.
3. Then, the puppy jumped around to get the man's attention.
4. Last, the man took home the puppy.

Summarize, pp. 57–60
Selection: Call 911, p. 59

1. If you need help, you can call 911, a special number set up for emergencies.
2. Possible answer: The operator will send the police, an ambulance, or the fire department to your address.
3. Possible answer: "Many lives have been saved by people calling 911 quickly in an emergency."

Graphic Organizer: How to Summarize, p. 60

Main Idea: If you need help, you can call 911.
Detail: The operator will ask for your name and address.
Detail: The operator will send help.
Detail: Dial "O" if your town doesn't have a 911 system.
Summary: Possible answer: If you have an emergency, call 911. The operator will ask for your information and send help. You can dial "0" if your town does not have 911.